DISCARD

7/03

Forces in action

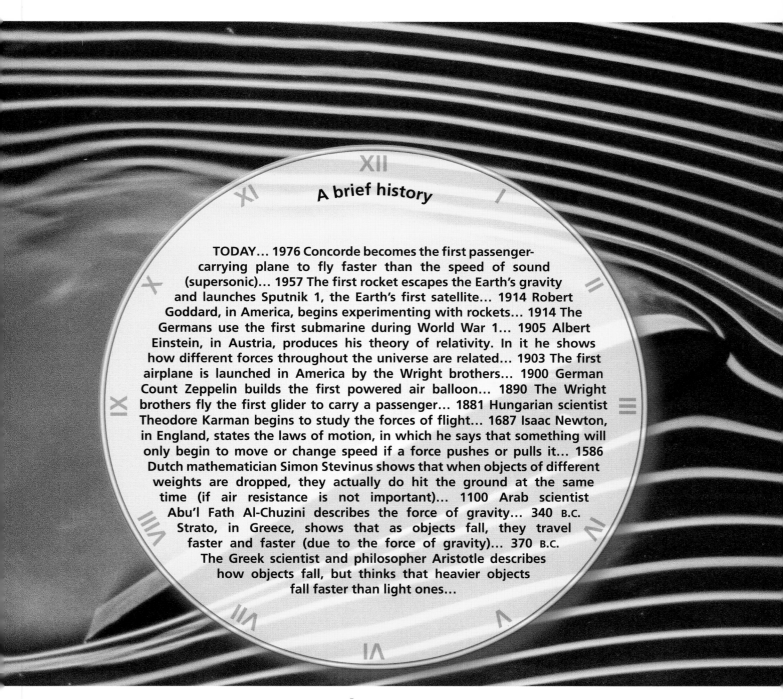

A brief history

TODAY... 1976 Concorde becomes the first passenger-carrying plane to fly faster than the speed of sound (supersonic)... 1957 The first rocket escapes the Earth's gravity and launches Sputnik 1, the Earth's first satellite... 1914 Robert Goddard, in America, begins experimenting with rockets... 1914 The Germans use the first submarine during World War 1... 1905 Albert Einstein, in Austria, produces his theory of relativity. In it he shows how different forces throughout the universe are related... 1903 The first airplane is launched in America by the Wright brothers... 1900 German Count Zeppelin builds the first powered air balloon... 1890 The Wright brothers fly the first glider to carry a passenger... 1881 Hungarian scientist Theodore Karman begins to study the forces of flight... 1687 Isaac Newton, in England, states the laws of motion, in which he says that something will only begin to move or change speed if a force pushes or pulls it... 1586 Dutch mathematician Simon Stevinus shows that when objects of different weights are dropped, they actually do hit the ground at the same time (if air resistance is not important)... 1100 Arab scientist Abu'l Fath Al-Chuzini describes the force of gravity... 340 B.C. Strato, in Greece, shows that as objects fall, they travel faster and faster (due to the force of gravity)... 370 B.C. The Greek scientist and philosopher Aristotle describes how objects fall, but thinks that heavier objects fall faster than light ones...

Dr. Brian Knapp

Word list

These are some science words that you should look out for as you go through the book. They are shown using CAPITAL letters.

BUOYANCY
The tendency of an object to float or to rise when submerged.

CENTER OF GRAVITY
The place on an object at which it can be balanced.

DENSE, DENSITY
The compactness of a substance. How dense a substance is depends on how much of it is in a given volume.

FLOAT
To rest on the surface of a liquid or in a gas.

FORCE
A push or a pull that causes a movement to take place. If something is already moving, it can cause it to speed up or slow down.

FORCE METER
An instrument designed to measure a force.

GRAVITY
The force that attracts one body to another. It acts everywhere in the universe. The gravitational force depends on the size and the density of an object. So, for an object the size of a marble the gravitational force is too small to notice. But for an object the size of the Earth it is very large. We are pulled toward the center of the Earth by its gravitational force. In turn the Earth is pulled toward the Sun by the Sun's huge gravitational force.

LEVER
A device for moving a heavy load using a small force.

LIFTING FORCE
The upward force, or lift, that acts on something traveling quickly through the air.

NEWTON
The unit of force. When measuring weights, a newton is about a tenth of a kilogram.

ORBIT
The path followed by a planet as it moves around the Sun.

PIVOT
The balancing point of a beam or any other kind of lever.

PROJECTILE
An object propelled through the air.

REACTION
A force, such as a push or pull, that opposes an action. Friction is a common reaction force.

SUBMERGE
To sink under the water.

WEIGHT
A force produced by gravity acting on an object. It can be measured in newtons or kilograms (or pounds).

WEIGHTLESSNESS
A state in which the force of gravity is very small, or in which gravity is balanced by another force, such as fast movement.

Contents

	Page

Forces all around us

Everything is acted on by forces, even if, for much of the time, we do not notice it.

If you push a thumbtack into a piece of wood, the sharp point of the tack will sink into the wood (Picture 1). What you have done is to use **FORCE** to push the tack into the wood. Pushing is one kind of force.

If you drag a log along the ground (Picture 2) or use a trolley to lift a heavy box, you use another kind of force—a pulling force.

You can pick up small iron and steel objects with a magnet (Picture 3) or pull hair upright using a comb charged with electricity (Picture 4). These are two more kinds of force.

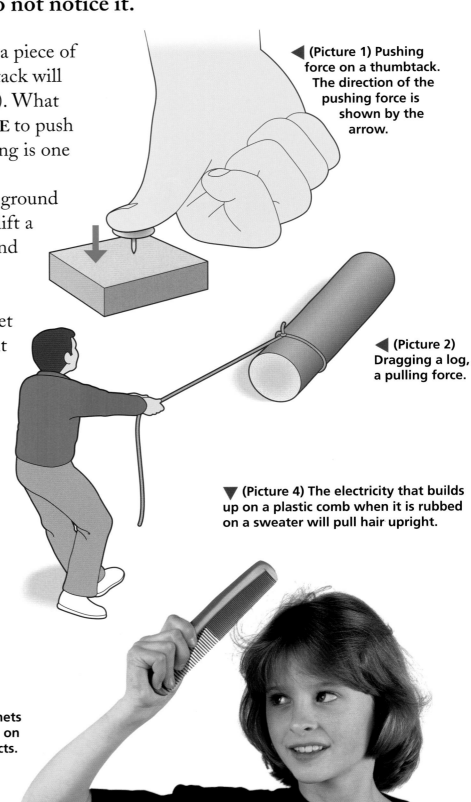

◄ (Picture 1) Pushing force on a thumbtack. The direction of the pushing force is shown by the arrow.

◄ (Picture 2) Dragging a log, a pulling force.

▼ (Picture 4) The electricity that builds up on a plastic comb when it is rubbed on a sweater will pull hair upright.

◄ (Picture 3) Magnets have magnetic pull on iron and steel objects.

If the driver of a car wants to go faster, he or she presses down on the accelerator. That causes the engine to apply more force to the wheels. The change in speed is caused by a change in the force.

So, a force is something that gets an object moving or, if it is already moving, changes its speed or direction.

Action and reaction

Press on a thumbtack. As you begin to push down, the wood presses back up against your thumb. That is another, opposing, force.

▲ **(Picture 5) The LIFTING FORCE is a reaction to the downward push of the powerful engines.**

When a space shuttle takes off, the rocket engines push out huge amounts of gas (Picture 5). The gases move down, and the rocket moves up.

These examples show that forces always work in pairs (Picture 6). The force that causes movement always produces an opposing force that we call a **REACTION**.

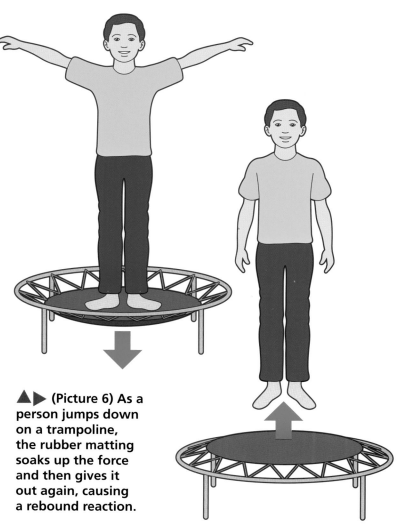

▲▶ **(Picture 6) As a person jumps down on a trampoline, the rubber matting soaks up the force and then gives it out again, causing a rebound reaction.**

Summary
- A force is a push, a pull, or a change in speed or direction.
- Forces work in pairs; a force is always opposed by a reaction.

Force meter

A FORCE METER is an instrument that measures a pulling or pushing force. Scales are force meters for measuring weight.

A force, such as pulling or pushing, will make something go faster or slower, make it go in a new direction, or change its shape. For example, we might drag a chair across a room. That uses pulling force. We might squash a ball. We use force to do that too.

Measuring force

The more force we use when pulling something, such as a rubber band, the more it will stretch. We can use this principle to make a simple instrument for measuring force (Picture 1).

Each extra weight in the pan adds to the force stretching the rubber band. The more force we use, the more the band stretches, and the further the pointer moves down the scale.

In this example we have used weight as a force, but we could turn the instrument on its side to measure the force when pulling sideways.

Force meter

A force meter is a tube containing a spring and a pointer. The force meter can be used for measuring forces downward or sideways (Picture 2). It can also be used for measuring pushes as well as pulls. The scale on a force meter is marked off in units of force called **NEWTONS**.

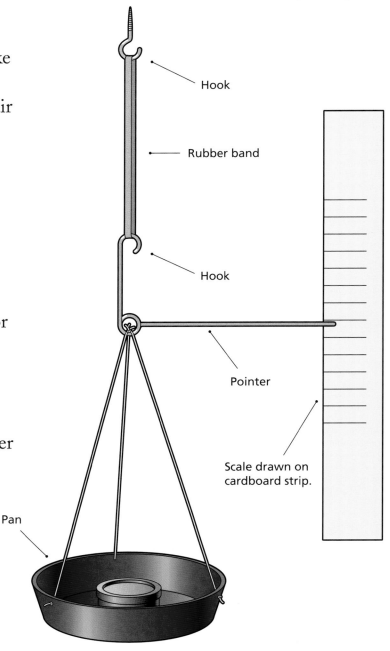

Hook

Rubber band

Hook

Pointer

Scale drawn on cardboard strip.

Pan

▲ **(Picture 1) You can make your own instrument for measuring downward force by attaching a small pan and a pointer to a rubber band. Place a piece of cardboard next to the pointer.**
Put a 100g weight in the pan, and mark 1 newton (1N) where the pointer comes on the scale. Add 100g more, and mark 2N where the pointer shows. By adding more weights, you can make a scale.

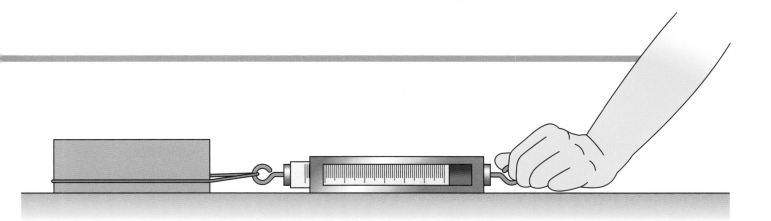

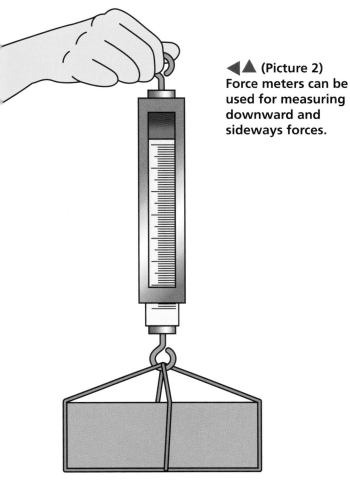

◀▲ (Picture 2) Force meters can be used for measuring downward and sideways forces.

Force meters around us

Stores use scales for finding the **WEIGHT** before selling you goods such as apples or potatoes (Picture 3). These scales are not marked in newtons but in kilograms (and for smaller weights, grams). Newtons is a more general unit that can be used for sideways and upward pushes and pulls, as well as downward pulls. (Kilograms can only be used for weight. A kilo is about 10 newtons.)

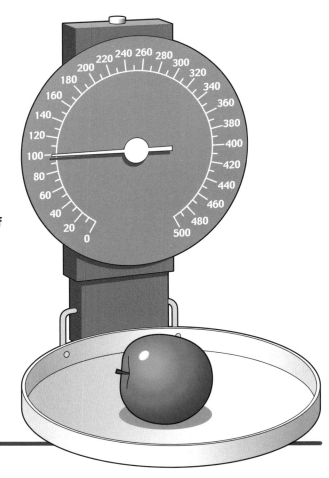

▶ (Picture 3) Weighing scales are a common kind of force meter. The scale in this picture shows that the apple weighs 100g, which is also a force of about 1 newton (1,000g or 1kg is about 10 newtons).

Summary

- A force meter measures pulling force.
- Force is measured in newtons.
- When measuring weight, a kilogram is about 10 newtons.

Gravity

One of the most common forces is GRAVITY. It is the force that pulls us toward the center of the Earth and pulls the planets toward the Sun.

We take the biggest force in our lives completely for granted. It is the force of the Earth pulling us to its center. We call it gravity.

We measure gravity through weight, as we saw on page 7. Gravity is a force created by the size of an object in space and our closeness to it. In space, where we are not close to the Earth or another planet, there is little gravity (Picture 1). Here, apples would weigh almost nothing. On the Moon, which is a much smaller body, gravity is only a sixth as powerful as on Earth. Apples that weighed 1,200g on Earth would weigh just 200g (a sixth of 1,200, or 1,200 divided by six) on the Moon.

▲ (Picture 1) If gravity were taken away, there would be no force pulling us, and we would simply FLOAT around. This is called WEIGHTLESSNESS, and it is what astronauts experience in space.

Weightlessness is not good for the body. Our muscles are always working against gravity, lifting our arms and legs and moving us around, and that is what keeps the muscles and bones of our bodies strong. In space, with such small forces to resist our movements, bones and muscles have little work to do, and they are weakened.

The use of gravity

Gravity is very important to us. It pulls us toward the ground and keeps us from floating off into space. Gravity pulls your breakfast cereal to the bottom of its bowl, pulls your computer down on the table, pulls the table on the floor, and so on.

The problem with gravity

Gravity is not always useful. It keeps athletes from being able to jump very high off the ground. It makes it very hard for planes to fly and even harder for rockets to leave the Earth completely.

Gravity also makes things fall very quickly; so if brakes fail on a car when it is on a slope, the car will quickly gain speed and may crash, with unpleasant effects.

Gravity holds our solar system together

Everything has a gravitational pull. The amount of the pull depends on its size. The Earth has a larger gravitational force than the Moon because it is bigger. However, the Earth is small compared to the Sun, and so the gravitational force of the Earth is tiny compared to that of the Sun.

The Sun's gravity is so strong that all of the planets are pulled toward it (Picture 2). What keeps them all from colliding with the Sun? The fact that they are moving very fast. If the Sun stopped pulling on the planets, they would all fly off into space. In this case the force that tries to make planets fly into space is balanced by the gravity force that pulls them toward the Sun. Because the forces are in balance, all of the planets remain the same distance from the Sun, getting neither closer nor further away.

Summary

- **Gravity is a force.**
- **Weight is caused by gravity acting on things.**
- **Gravity depends on the size of objects in space; things weigh less on the Moon than on the Earth.**

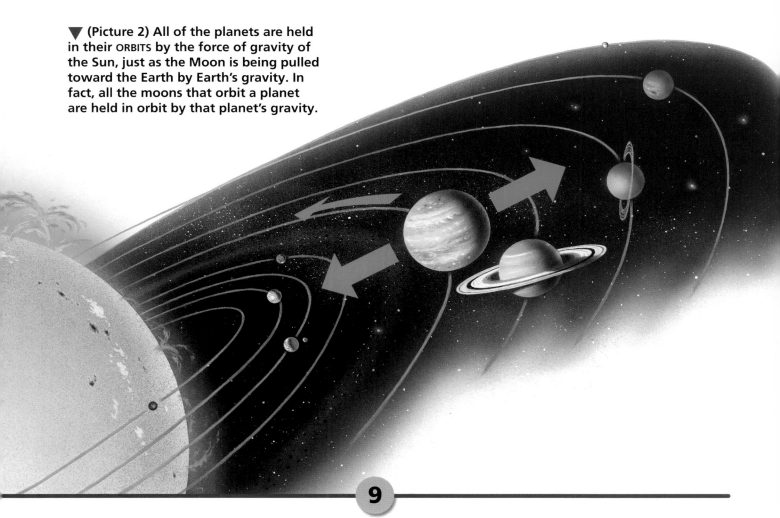

▼ (Picture 2) All of the planets are held in their ORBITS by the force of gravity of the Sun, just as the Moon is being pulled toward the Earth by Earth's gravity. In fact, all the moons that orbit a planet are held in orbit by that planet's gravity.

Forces that balance

If forces are balanced, nothing moves.

If there are forces all around, why are most things stationary? The answer is that the force trying to cause movement (such as gravity) is usually resisted by a force of equal size.

For example, you don't break through the seat of your chair because it is strong enough to resist your weight. The chair can push back up as much as you push down. The forces are balanced. Sit an elephant on your chair, and things might be different, however.

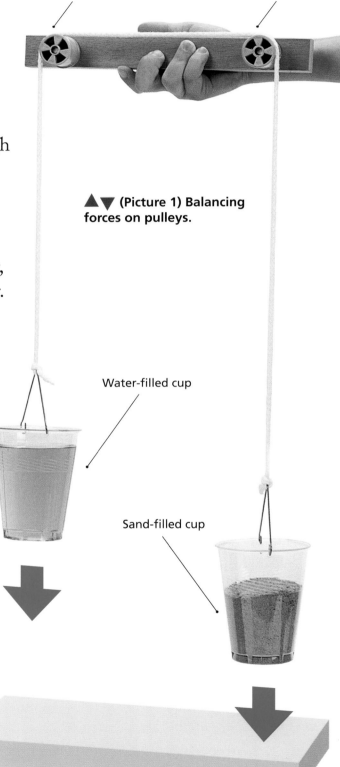

▲▼ **(Picture 1) Balancing forces on pulleys.**

Water-filled cup

Sand-filled cup

Finding a balance

You know things are in balance when they do not move. In Picture 1 you can see a pair of plastic cups connected by a string over two pulleys. One cup contains sand, and water is being added to the other cup. At this moment nothing is moving. The sand-filled cup is as heavy as the water-filled

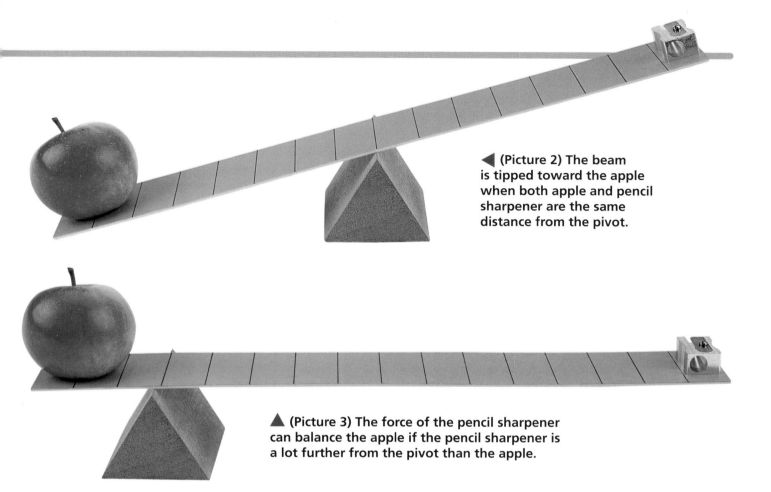

◀ (Picture 2) The beam is tipped toward the apple when both apple and pencil sharpener are the same distance from the pivot.

▲ (Picture 3) The force of the pencil sharpener can balance the apple if the pencil sharpener is a lot further from the pivot than the apple.

cup, and so both are still. The water-filled cup is pulling against the sand-filled cup, but not enough to cause movement. When more water is added, the force on the water-filled cup will get bigger, and the cups will be out of balance. As a result, the sand-filled cup will rise.

Small force, large distance

In Picture 2 a cardboard "beam" rests on a sharp-edged block of wood. The sharp edge is a **PIVOT**. It allows the beam to rock on it.

Here the apple and the pencil sharpener are the *same distance* from the pivot. The apple is heavier, so the beam tips down until the apple end is resting on the table.

In Picture 3 the pivot has been moved close to the apple. Strangely, the tiny pencil sharpener can now balance the heavy apple. To do this, the downward force of the pencil sharpener must be balancing the downward force of the apple. That is possible because the force depends not just on the weight but also on the distance from the pivot.

This is a way of moving heavy objects with little force. You will see more of this on the next page. It is the principle of how a **LEVER** works.

Summary
• When something is balanced, the forces are equal.
• A small force can balance a large force by using a pivot; the small force must be farther from the pivot than the large force.

Levers

A lever is designed to make it easier for you to lift, cut, or squeeze.

A lever is something that multiplies force. The simplest lever is a bar, but there are many kinds of levers. Even a screw is a lever!

How a lever works

Picture 1 shows the sort of long, hooked bar used to get nails out of wood. You would never get a nail out of wood by using your fingers. What you need to do is to multiply your force. You do this with a long bar.

When you use a bar like this, you pivot the bar close to the thing you want to move. In this case the bend in the bar is used as the pivot.

The longer, the better

When you use a lever, the further you are from the pivot, the more your force is multiplied. So the longer the lever is, the more powerful it can be.

The ancient Greek scientist Archimedes once said, "Give me a long enough lever, and I could move the Earth." In theory this is true, but of course, he would also have needed a pivot somewhere in space.

Many kinds of pivot

The key to using a lever is the pivot. Picture 2 shows you a person using a plank to move a large log. Notice that the plank rests on a smaller log and that the small log (the pivot) is close to the large log. To see how it works, compare it to Picture 1.

Picture 3 shows a pair of scissors. In this case there are two levers attached together. The pivot is where they are fastened. You can see the importance of

Pulling force

Pivot

Object to be moved

◀ **(Picture 1) You would not be able to pull a nail out with your fingers, but it is easy with a lever.**

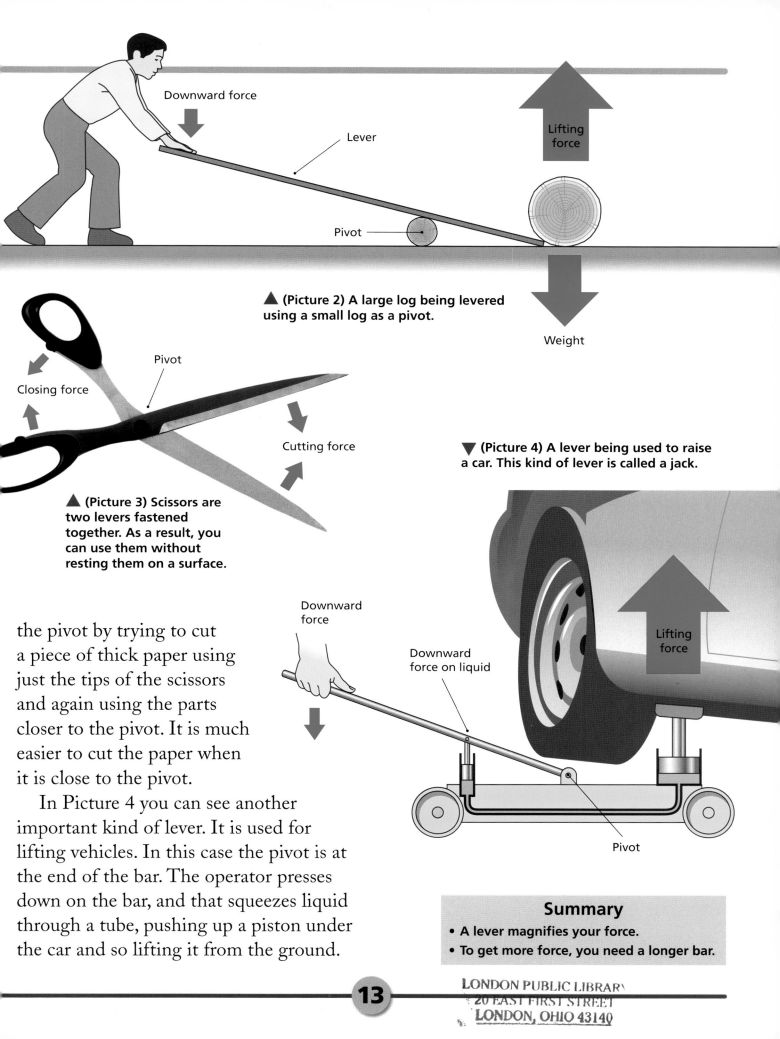

Downward force

Lever

Lifting force

Pivot

▲ (Picture 2) A large log being levered using a small log as a pivot.

Weight

Pivot

Closing force

Cutting force

▲ (Picture 3) Scissors are two levers fastened together. As a result, you can use them without resting them on a surface.

▼ (Picture 4) A lever being used to raise a car. This kind of lever is called a jack.

Downward force

Downward force on liquid

Lifting force

Pivot

the pivot by trying to cut a piece of thick paper using just the tips of the scissors and again using the parts closer to the pivot. It is much easier to cut the paper when it is close to the pivot.

In Picture 4 you can see another important kind of lever. It is used for lifting vehicles. In this case the pivot is at the end of the bar. The operator presses down on the bar, and that squeezes liquid through a tube, pushing up a piston under the car and so lifting it from the ground.

Summary
- A lever magnifies your force.
- To get more force, you need a longer bar.

13

Center of gravity

The CENTER OF GRAVITY is the place where all of an object's weight balances.

Have you ever wondered why a spoon balances on your finger? And why will it only balance with the bowl end nearer your finger (Picture 1)?

The answer to both of these questions is because of forces.

When the spoon is in balance, the forces pulling down on one side equal the forces pulling down on the other (Picture 2). In this case the force is the invisible force of gravity. We call the place where an object will balance "the center of gravity." The center of gravity of the balancing spoon is exactly where it touches the finger, that is, on the pivot.

Finding the center of gravity

We can find out the center of gravity of any object by trial and error. We keep trying to balance it at different places until it stays at rest. This is quite easy to do with a spoon, but more difficult

▲ (Picture 1) An object will balance if you can place it over its center of gravity.

▼ (Picture 2) Because these baskets are the same weight, the pivot point is halfway along the rod and over the woman's shoulder. This allows her to balance the weights and so carry them easily.

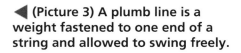

◀ (Picture 3) A plumb line is a weight fastened to one end of a string and allowed to swing freely.

for complicated shapes. We can use a plumb line (Picture 3) to help us find the center of gravity, or balancing point, of any object.

Picture 4 shows how to find the center of gravity of an irregular object, in this case a letter A that has been cut out of cardboard.

▼ **(Picture 4) Finding the center of gravity of an object using a plumb line. Suspend the plumb line and object from the same pin so they swing freely. Let them come to rest, then mark the position of the string.**
Repeat this at two other places on the object. The center of gravity is where the lines cross.

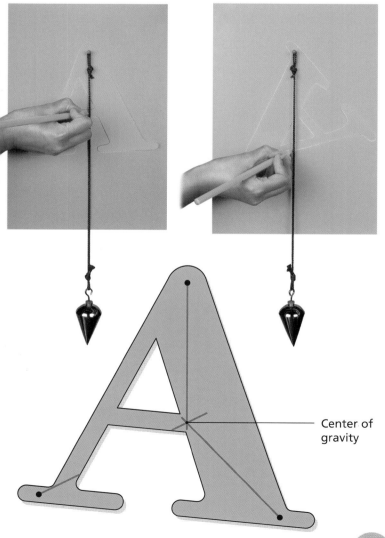

Center of gravity

Making use of the center of gravity

It is often useful to know where a center of gravity is so that an object can be made stable. A dune buggy, for example, has a low center of gravity so that it does not roll over when it turns a corner (Picture 5). If most of the weight of an object is high up, then the object is top-heavy and is likely to topple over easily.

▲▶ **(Picture 5) These are objects with low and high centers of gravity. The dune buggy has a low center of gravity and is less likely to fall over than the leaning tower of Pisa.**

Summary
- **The center of gravity is the place where the weight of an object balances.**
- **A lower center of gravity makes an object less liable to topple over.**

Floating

If something FLOATS, it means that the force pressing down is balanced by the force pressing up.

If you tie a brick to a force meter and then lower the brick into water, something extraordinary happens—the brick weighs less (Picture 1)!

You can try this with any object, and you will get the same result; the object weighs less when placed in water. We say things are "buoyed up" by the water.

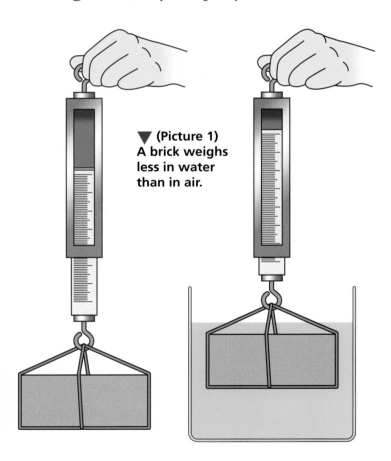

▼ (Picture 1) A brick weighs less in water than in air.

Floating

Things weigh less in water than in air because water is "thicker" (**DENSER**) than air.

For example, when you put a brick in water, it pushes some of the water away. However, the water presses back against the space it was pushed out of. This is called **BUOYANCY**.

Because the brick presses down more than the water pushes back, the brick sinks. But in many other cases objects do not push down as hard, and so they do not sink. Instead, they float.

As a general rule, the more dense something is, the more likely it is to sink. A piece of Plasticine made into a ball, for example, will sink through water. But even dense materials can be made to float. If the Plasticine ball is squashed into a sheet and then shaped into a boat, it will float (Picture 2). That is because the boat is now a combination of very light air and dense Plasticine. The Plasticine boat is,

▶ (Picture 2) Plasticine is denser than water. Made into a ball, it sinks. But made into a boat, it floats because the inside now contains air, which is less dense than Plasticine. The downward force of the air plus the force of the Plasticine can now be balanced by the upward force of the water.

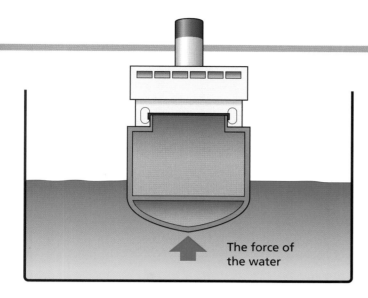

The force of the water

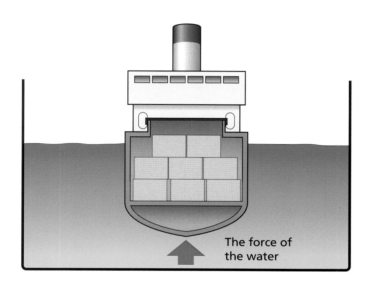

The force of the water

overall, less dense than water. In a similar way a real ship made of steel is, overall, still able to float (Picture 3).

Floating and density

Thick (dense) liquids push back more than thin ones. As a result, heavy things will float in a dense liquid but sink in a less dense liquid (Picture 4). For example, the Dead Sea contains a huge amount of salt. As a result, it is much denser than ordinary water. That is why no one can sink in it—even if they can't swim.

◀ (Picture 3) A ship floats high or low depending on what it contains. If it contains mainly air, it will float high in the water. If it is carrying cargo (which is heavier than air), it will float lower.

▼ (Picture 4) Whether something floats or sinks depends on how dense it is. Water will float on syrup because it is less dense than syrup. Oil will float on water because it is less dense than water. A carrot will sink in oil and water because it is more dense than both. But a carrot will float on syrup because it is less dense than syrup. Balsa wood or a cork will float on oil because they are less dense than syrup, water, and oil. A steel screw is more dense than the liquids, and so it will sink through all of them.

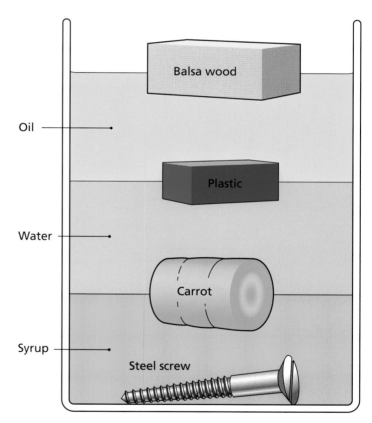

Oil

Water

Syrup

Balsa wood

Plastic

Carrot

Steel screw

Summary
• Water and other liquids support solids.
• If a solid is light enough, it will float.
• Some heavy materials are made light enough to float by making them hollow.

Submerged

Moving around while SUBMERGED is more difficult than floating.

If you are more dense ("heavier") than water, you sink. If you are less dense ("lighter"), you float. But what if you want to move around underwater?

Sea creatures

The sea is full of creatures that can move around in the water. Some, such as sharks, are actually heavier than water; if they stop moving around, they sink to the bottom. But most fish have an air-filled bag inside them (Picture 1). It helps make them about the same density as the water around them. However, they cannot change the amount of air in this bag. If they want to go up or down in the water, they have to keep swimming, just as we do.

The nautilus can float or sink in water by changing its density (Picture 2). This creature has many chambers inside its shell. To rise in the water, it fills its chambers with air; to sink, it fills the chambers with water.

How submarines work

Submarines rise and fall in the water using the principle of the nautilus (Picture 3). They have two hulls, and the space between the inner and outer hull can be filled with either water or air.

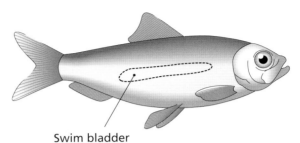

Swim bladder

▲ **(Picture 1)** A fish can remain still in the water because it has an air-filled bag (called a swim bladder) that is used to counteract its weight and make the fish just about the same density as water.

▲ **(Picture 2)** Ancient sea creatures like the ammonites and modern creatures like the nautilus can increase and reduce their buoyancy by filling chambers in their shells with either air or water.

If it is filled with water, the submarine becomes denser than water and sinks. If the water is pumped out, the submarine becomes lighter than water and rises.

A model diving straw shows how this works (Picture 4).

▼ (Picture 3) The depth of a submarine is changed by filling or emptying special water tanks between the hulls.

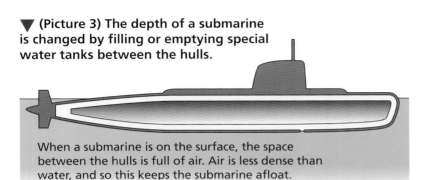

When a submarine is on the surface, the space between the hulls is full of air. Air is less dense than water, and so this keeps the submarine afloat.

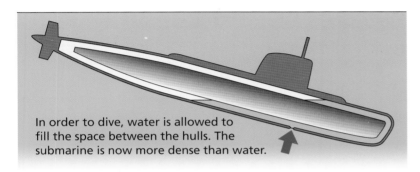

In order to dive, water is allowed to fill the space between the hulls. The submarine is now more dense than water.

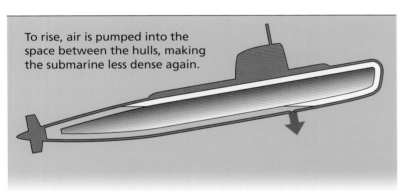

To rise, air is pumped into the space between the hulls, making the submarine less dense again.

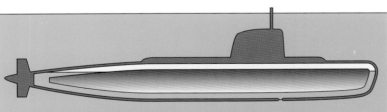

By adjusting the amount of water and air in the hulls, the submarine can be made the same density as the water around it. It will then neither sink nor float.

Summary

- To stay submerged in water but not sink, an object needs to have the same density as water.
- You can change the depth of a submerged object by changing the amount of water or air in the object.

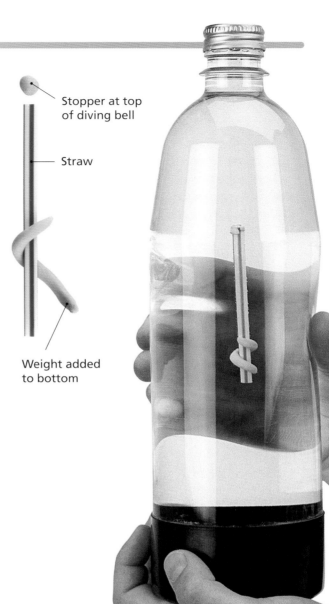

Stopper at top of diving bell

Straw

Weight added to bottom

▲ (Picture 4) You can make a straw diving bell that will rise and fall in a plastic bottle. To adjust the straw's buoyancy, plug the top with Plasticine or putty. Place the straw in a bowl of water, and add or remove Plasticine on the bottom of the straw until the straw just floats upright with the top on the surface of the water.

Next, completely fill a plastic bottle with water, add the straw vertically so that air is kept inside it, and screw on the bottle cap. When you squeeze the bottle, the water is squashed, and some of the water goes up the inside of the straw, making it heavier. As a result, it sinks. Releasing the bottle makes the straw rise.

The force of the air

Air can slow things down, but fast-moving air can also be an important lifting force.

Air is all around us, but we don't normally think about it as a force. That is because air is a "thin" substance that is easily pushed out of the way as we walk around. But if an object moves quickly through the air, then the air does not move out of the way fast enough, and so it acts as a force that holds back, or resists, that movement.

Parachute

A feather or a parachute seed drops slowly through the air because it is light and has a large area to trap the air (Picture 1).

You can see how a large area makes an object fall more slowly by making a parachute from a piece of paper, some cotton threads, and a weight (Picture 2).

Lifting force of the air

◀▼ (Picture 2) A parachute falls slowly because the large surface area traps the air, making it difficult for the air to flow out of the way. In this case the weight is always greater than the air resistance, so the parachute falls no matter how big it is.

Weight of parachute

▼ (Picture 1) Some seeds act as natural parachutes.

Making air cause lift

We have seen how air can stop movement, but it can also be used to lift things off the ground. For example, a hovercraft works by forcing air at high speed into a hollow space below the craft. The air gets squashed up and pushes against the ground and the craft (Picture 3). The air is used to hold the craft off the ground.

Air pressure lifts wing

Weight of wing

▼ (Picture 3) You can show how hovercraft work by squashing air. Simply glue a paper tube over a hole in a shoebox, and blow. The hovercraft will rise. In this case the force of the air pressure is greater than the weight of the shoebox lid.

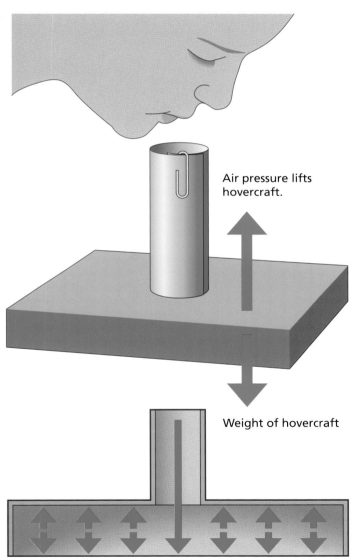

Air pressure lifts hovercraft.

Weight of hovercraft

▲ (Picture 4) You can show the lifting force of a wing by folding over a piece of paper and gluing it to make a wing. Thread it through a string, and walk quickly forward. The air will give lifting force. In this case the lifting force is greater than the weight of the wing, so the wing moves.

An aircraft also gets its lift from the air. It is pushed forward through the air at high speed by its engines. As it moves, the air builds up more pressure under the wing than above it. That creates an upward force we call lift or **LIFTING FORCE**. It is an easy thing to demonstrate (Picture 4).

Summary
- Air becomes a force when it is squashed.
- Lifting force is a force that works when things move quickly through air.

Throwing things

When you throw something in the air, it goes up and down, and also travels sideways.

Do you know how to throw a ball or a stone the greatest distance? Do you throw it high in the air, send it close to the ground, or throw it somewhere between these two?

When something is thrown through the air, it is called a **PROJECTILE**. It goes up as high as it can, then falls down. At the same time, it is moving sideways (Picture 1).

If you throw a ball straight up, all of your force is used up in making the ball go up, and almost none is used to make it go sideways at all. It gets very high in the air, but doesn't go sideways.

If you throw it sideways, you put all of your force into making it go sideways as far as it will go, but very little force is used to make it go up.

Cannon

In the days of cannon the problem of how to aim was just like throwing. The amount of gunpowder (which produced the force) was always the same, so the distance the ball could reach depended on the angle at which it was fired. Picture 2 shows a simple way of finding out what angle throws a projectile the greatest distance. In this case the angle of the ramp changes, but the stretch of the rubber band (the force) is always the same.

▼ (Picture 1) How far a ball, a cannonball, a stone, or any other object travels depends on how hard it is thrown and the angle it is thrown at.

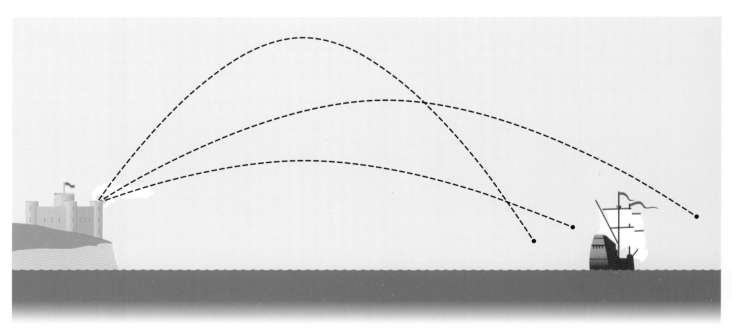

The effect of air

As the projectile flies through the air, the air resists it and slows it down. That may slightly change the angle that gives the furthest distance. The best angle for sending a projectile the furthest is 45 degrees, that is, half-way between the horizontal (sideways) and the vertical (straight up).

Ballister

The distance you can throw something depends on the force you use to throw it as well as the angle you throw it at. Picture 3 shows you how to make a medieval throwing machine called a ballister. The machine is designed so that when you press down gently on the front edge of the rod, the ball will be thrown into the air.

You can make a fair test of how far a ball will travel with different amounts of force by stretching the rubber band by different amounts. The different hooks allow for different amounts of stretch.

Rubber band provides force to pull the arm.

Hooks allow the tension on the rubber band to be adjusted. The more tension, the greater the force.

▶ (Picture 3) A ballister made from a sheet of plywood and a wooden dowel.

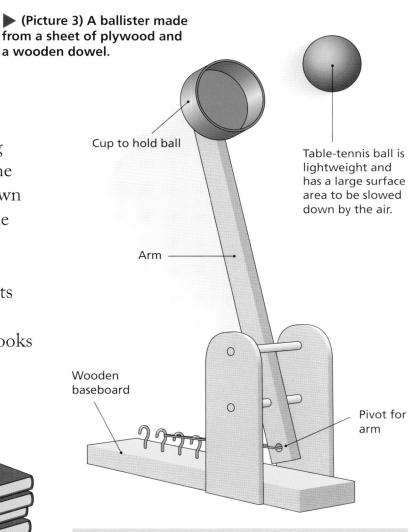

Cup to hold ball

Table-tennis ball is lightweight and has a large surface area to be slowed down by the air.

Arm

Wooden baseboard

Pivot for arm

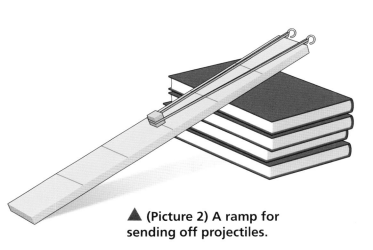

▲ (Picture 2) A ramp for sending off projectiles.

Summary

• Something that is thrown through the air is called a projectile.
• A projectile travels furthest when it is thrown from an angle of about 45 degrees.

Index

Science Matters!

Grolier Educational

First published in the United States in 2003 by Grolier Educational, Sherman Turnpike, Danbury, CT 06816

Copyright © 2003
Atlantic Europe Publishing Company Ltd.

All rights reserved. No part of this publication may be reproduced, stored in a retrieval system, or transmitted in any form or by any means—electronic, mechanical, photocopying, recording, or otherwise—without prior permission of the publisher.

This product is manufactured from sustainable managed forests. For every tree cut down at least one more is planted.

Author
Brian Knapp, BSc, PhD

Educational Consultant
Peter Riley, BSc, C Biol, MI Biol, PGCE

Art Director
Duncan McCrae, BSc

Senior Designer
Adele Humphries, BA, PGCE

Editor
Lisa Magloff, BA

Illustrations
David Woodroffe

Designed and produced by
Earthscape Editions

Reproduced in Malaysia by
Global Color

Printed in Hong Kong by
Wing King Tong Company Ltd

Picture credits
All photographs are from the Earthscape Editions photolibrary, except the following: (c=center t=top b=bottom l=left r=right) NASA Cover (Astronauts James S. Voss and James M. Kelly on board the International Space Station's U.S. laboratory Destiny), 5tr, 8tr.

Library of Congress Cataloging-in-Publication Data
Knapp, Dr. Brian J.
    Science Matters! / [Dr. Brian J. Knapp].
        p. cm.
    Includes index.
    Summary: Presents information on a wide variety of topics in basic biology, chemistry, and physics.
    Contents: v. 1. Food, teeth, and eating—v. 2. Helping plants grow well—v. 3. Properties of materials—v. 4. Rocks and soils—v. 5. Springs and magnets—v. 6. Light and shadows—v. 7. Moving and growing—v. 8. Habitats—v. 9. Keeping warm and cool—v. 10. Solids and liquids—v. 11. Friction—v. 12. Simple electricity—v. 13. Keeping healthy—v. 14. Life cycles—v. 15. Gases around us—v. 16. Changing from solids to liquids to gases—v. 17. Earth and beyond—v. 18. Changing sounds—v. 19. Adapting and surviving—v. 20. Microbes—v. 21. Dissolving—v. 22. Changing materials—v. 23. Forces in action—v. 24. How we see things—v. 25. Changing circuits.
    ISBN 0-7172-5834-3 (set)—ISBN 0-7172-5835-1 (v. 1)—ISBN 0-7172-5836-X (v. 2)—ISBN 0-7172-5837-8 (v. 3)—ISBN 0-7172-5838-6 (v. 4)—ISBN 0-7172-5839-4 (v. 5)—ISBN 0-7172-5840-8 (v. 6)—ISBN 0-7172-5841-6 (v. 7)—ISBN 0-7172-5842-4 (v. 8)—ISBN 0-7172-5843-2 (v. 9)—ISBN 0-7172-5844-0 (v. 10)—ISBN 0-7172-5845-9 (v. 11)—ISBN 0-7172-5846-7 (v. 12)—ISBN 0-7172-5847-5 (v. 13)—ISBN 0-7172-5848-3 (v. 14)—ISBN 0-7172-5849-1 (v. 15)—ISBN 0-7172-5850-5 (v. 16)—ISBN 0-7172-5851-3 (v. 17)—ISBN 0-7172-5852-1 (v. 18)—ISBN 0-7172-5853-X (v. 19)—ISBN 0-7172-5854-8 (v. 20)—ISBN 0-7172-5855-6 (v. 21)—ISBN 0-7172-5856-4 (v. 22)—ISBN 0-7172-5857-2 (v. 23)—ISBN 0-7172-5858-0 (v. 24)—ISBN 0-7172-5859-9 (v. 25)
    1. Science—Juvenile literature. [1. Science.] I. Title.

Q163.K48 2002
500—dc21

2002017302